Once Upon a Workday

Encouraging Tales of Resilience

Elizabeth Pich and Jonathan Kunz

Andrews McMeel
PUBLISHING®

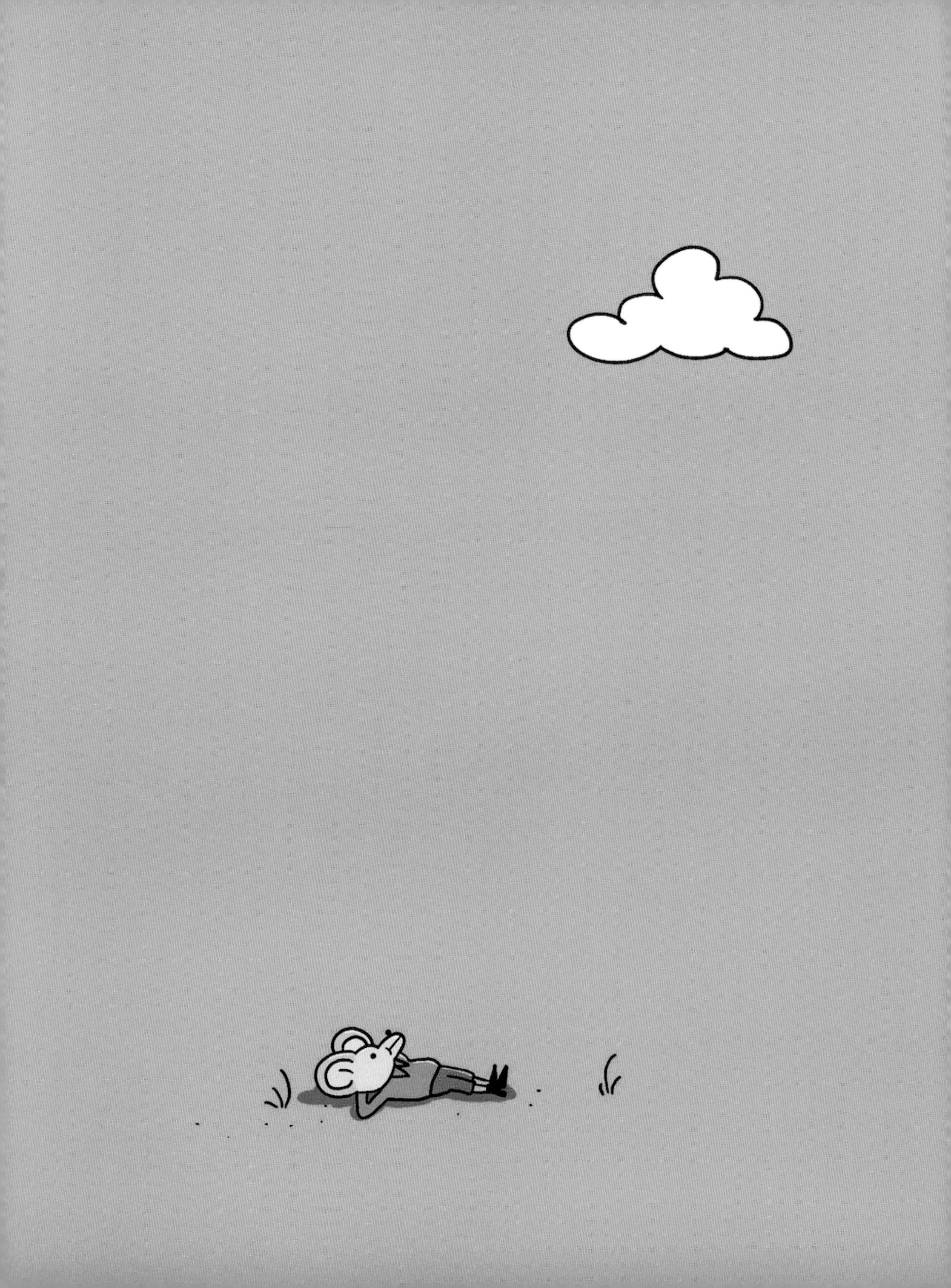

Once Upon A Workday

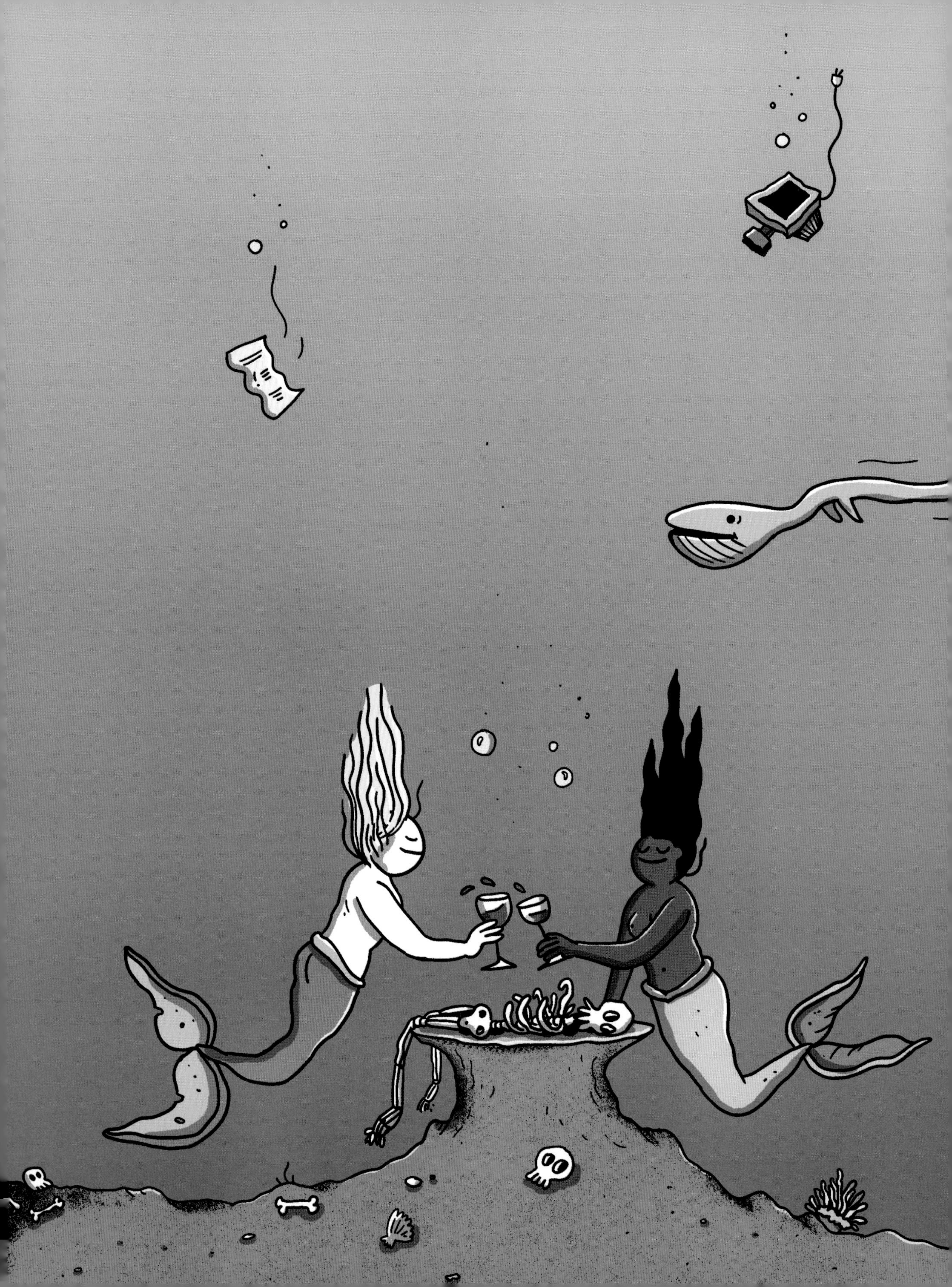

Contents

A Job Is a Job

Another day breaks, you pour out of bed.
Not a minute awake and in creeps the dread.

The gloom of the world waiting outside your door
With its deadlines, its meetings, its burdens, its chores!

You feel uninspired as you sit in your cube.
A few minutes of joy watching cat clips on YouTube.
When your colleagues ask a friendly *How do you do?*
You simply say *fine,* but you'd like to say *blue.*

You say to yourself, that's the way it must be!
There are duties and schedules and your kid's dentist fees.
A job is a job, and a job must be done!
There's no time to sit around and simply have fun!

So you slumpity-slump your way through each day.
And you gripe and you type as you labor away.

No, this will not do.
No, this simply won't do!
Who's running the show here?

It's you, my dear, **YOU**!

It's time to start asking what **you** want to do.

Plan some time for yourself, two, three hours a day.
Leave your smartphone at home, just go out and play!
Why did we ever stop playing? How silly, how wrong!
To think growing up means being serious all day long.

Remember, you liked to go out and dance?
And you once played guitar in that weird indie band.
Or painting—whatever did happen to that?
Strange how all of those passions fell flat.

Now a job is a job, and a job must be done.
But a you is a you, and you must also have fun.
So take a week off, one or two, six or eight!
This is your mental health—and that simply can't wait.

But wait! It's not easy when money is tight.
That's true, but you can still take that art course at night.
If risks aren't your thing, work part-time for a while.
In your newfound free time, do things that make you smile.

Taking care of yourself is the first job of all.
If you don't work at that, soon you'll have no job at all.
So eat a grand meal, sing a song, learn Malay.
Not just once in a while—do these things every day.

15

Yes, a job is a job, and a job must be done.

But taking care of yourself is job number one.

Night Party

At night when I lay on my most fluffy bed
And I'm ready to rest my most weary head.
My eyelids are heavy, they start their descent
Limbs snugly sprawled, neck finally unbent.

My whole self is quiet, not a sound to be heard.
Landscapes of matter to dreams are transferred.
Winds carry me seaward, I hear gasps of a carp.
I pick up from a distance the tones of the harp.

The songs of seraphim, yonder the clouds,
are luring me in with their snoozilous sounds.

But wait. I hear it. The tiniest blip!
Free thoughts are now fettered, I'm feeling the grip.
This blip, oh, I know it. It's a most dreadful tone.
It starts with one peep and then grows to a drone.

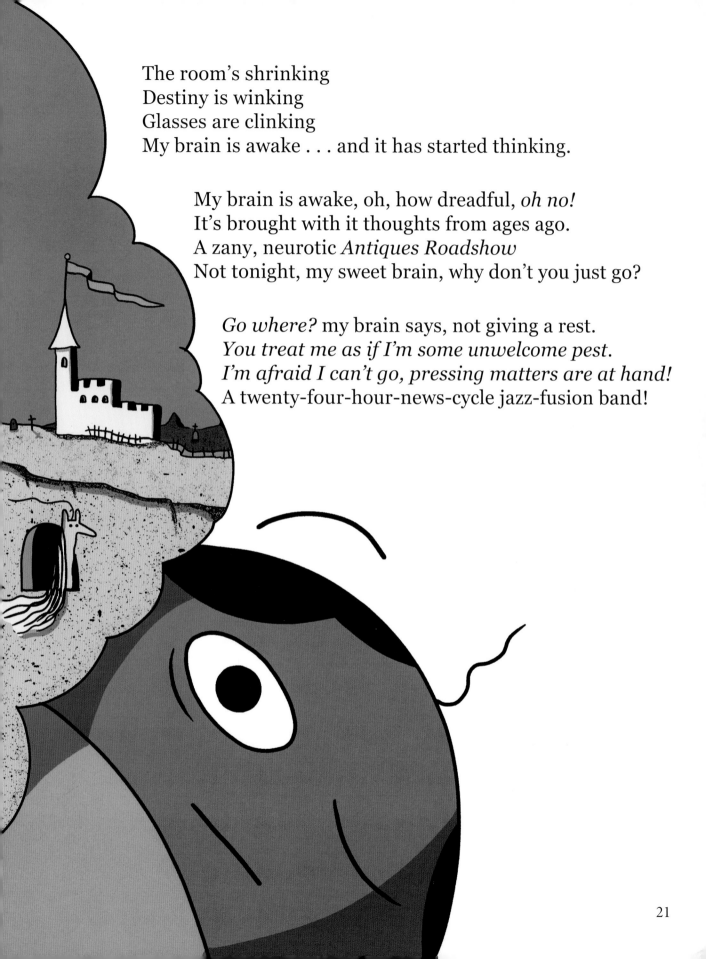

The room's shrinking
Destiny is winking
Glasses are clinking
My brain is awake . . . and it has started thinking.

My brain is awake, oh, how dreadful, *oh no!*
It's brought with it thoughts from ages ago.
A zany, neurotic *Antiques Roadshow*
Not tonight, my sweet brain, why don't you just go?

Go where? my brain says, not giving a rest.
You treat me as if I'm some unwelcome pest.
I'm afraid I can't go, pressing matters are at hand!
A twenty-four-hour-news-cycle jazz-fusion band!

I can try to sedate it, bonk myself on the head.
Or maybe a glass of warm milk instead.
Walk a few paces, count the holes in my sock.
Observe the alley cat's stroll down our block.

I meditate to the sweet song of wind chimes.
Let's rehash that awkward phone call seventeen times!
Some deep belly breathing. An affirmation or two.
Remember when that monkey stole your pants at the zoo?

Hark, that sliver of light—it's finally dawn.
Now we have to get up, you old nuisance, I yawn.

Oh dear, I'm quite tired! says my brain, so polite.
You'll have to make do without me, good night!

The Wandering Heart

My heart likes to wander
All over the place
Once it senses a blunder
It quickly gives chase

My heart likes to wander
Adrift on a cloud
I can't tell if it's thunder
Or my heart beating loud

At night when I slumber
I'm afraid it will break
But it still keeps on treading
Long after I wake

I worry my heart
Will beat right through my chest
I wish I could calm it
I can't take the stress!

Each day my heart wanders
Unwilling to rest
In search of lost love
On its eternal quest

The Artist's Lament

Hours and hours of work lay behind you.
Your weary bones ache and your head does, too.
There's crumpling and cramping in your legs, in your hand.
You risk falling over that old canvas stand.

It's time to take a step back and look at your jewel.
But you gasp out in horror, *oh,* you've been such a fool!
The trees look like trolls and the dogs look like sheep.
"Everything's come out wrong!" you slump down and weep.

Now it's all over! It's over, indeed!
When they said study law, you should have paid heed.
You've toiled away, all those years were in vain!
You might as well lay down and wait for the train.

You schlep yourself to bed, try to think of something nice.
But you see that ugly artwork every time you close your eyes.
Tomorrow you'll apply for that data-entry job.
Suffering in silence, like all those other sobs.

Sleep won't find you now, you're full of self-pity.
In vain, you try to meditate, read comics, pet your kitty.
So you get yourself up and—now you're feeling brash.
Those stupid inks and brushes are going straight into the trash.

But wait, what's that there? A mysterious pling.
A small silent chirp, a crisp ringing ring.
That corner right there, slightly catching my eye,
doesn't make me want to douse my whole place in lye.

That brushstroke up here, that's quite all right, too.
You don't outright love it, but it's not a pile of stinking poo.
You're sure you can mend it and make it great art!
You feel a fervent warmth warming up your heart.

You're right back on track, an unstoppable art machine.
Everybody will want to meet you—the pope and the queen!
This painting will sell for millions, your parents will be proud.
You can already hear the cheering and chanting of the crowd.

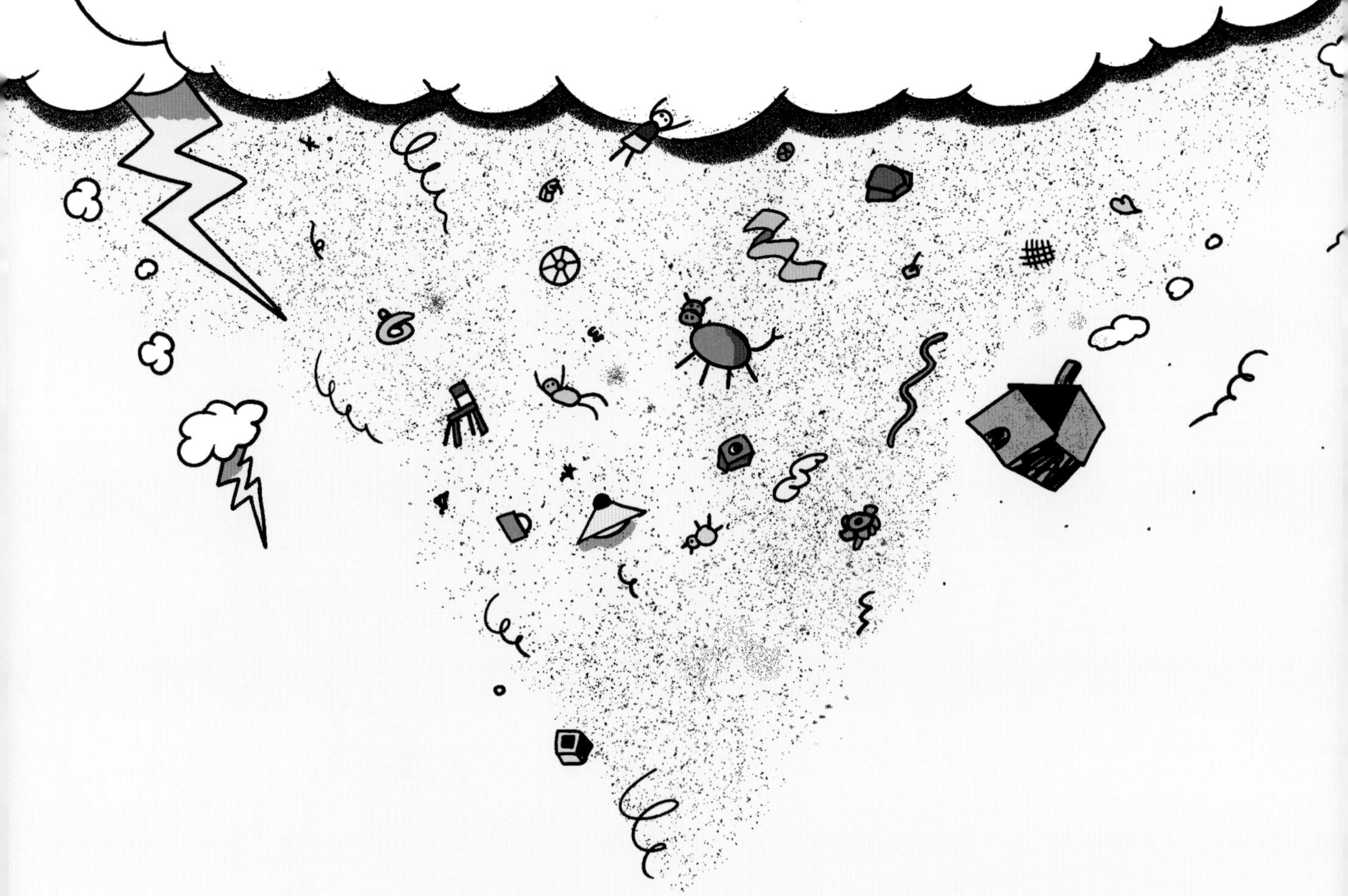

Some people call them brainstorms, for you it's hurricanes!
Pure creative genius is running through your veins.
Who's Picasso or Kahlo, who's Magritte or Monet?
Compared to yourself these old fogeys look gray.

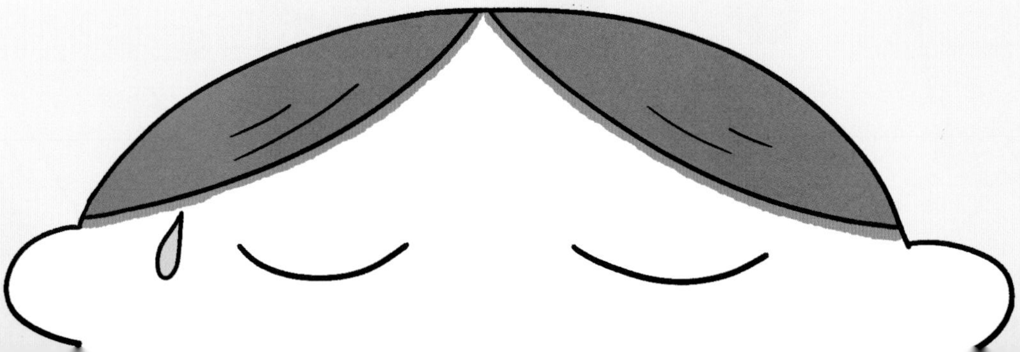

Now now there, young master. Don't get ahead of yourself!
You snicker, once again taking your brushes off the shelf.
Put your favorite record on, pour the coffee and the paint.
Let your thoughts flow with abandon, free of every constraint.

This project will take ages and your mind will feel vile.
But each grueling second will be worth your while.
If art is a scripture and you are its priest,
Then ideas are the flour and the grind is its yeast.

One hour later, the sun's coming out.
Your eyes are all crunchy, you're sure you've got gout.
Time to inspect your epic brushstroke ballet!
You take a look at your canvas and simply think: *Meh.*

You sink down the wall, time to hoist the white flag.
Maybe art is the boxer and you're the punching bag?
Now you're being dramatic, you must hit the brakes.
You're done for the day, and it's time for pancakes.

Sincerely Yours

I'm writing an email in the blandest of ways.
The wording is proper, the subject line is okay.
It's ready to send, I spent ages composing.
The only thing missing is the email's closing.

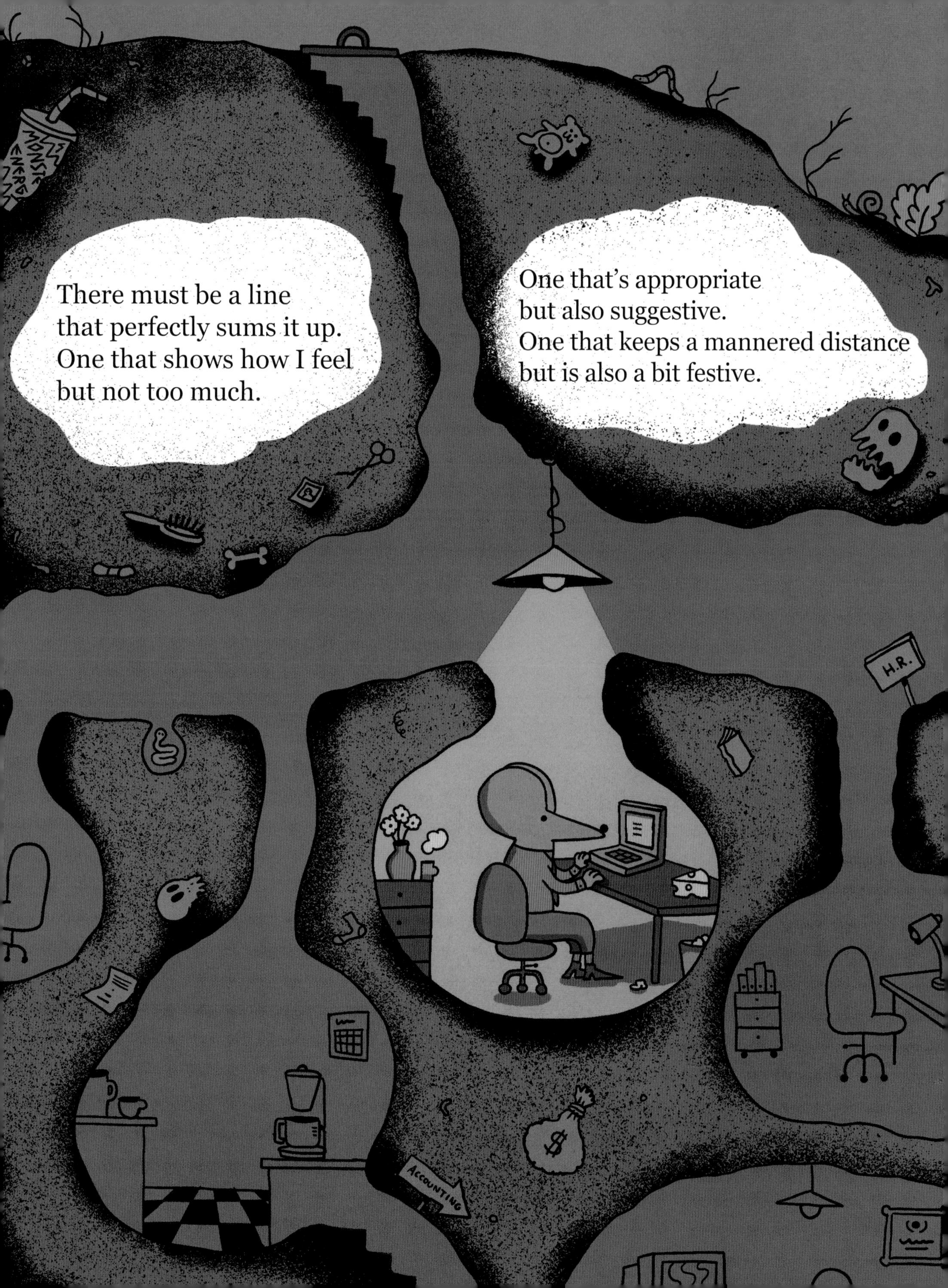
There must be a line
that perfectly sums it up.
One that shows how I feel
but not too much.
One that's appropriate
but also suggestive.
One that keeps a mannered distance
but is also a bit festive.
H.R.
ACCOUNTING

The whole perception of me
depends on this closing phrase.
A roundup of my traits,
the most meaningful glaze.

Sincerely yours might be right
but *Yours sincerely* sounds more British.
I want to show I'm not fickle
and most definitely not skittish.

Warm regards are nice but maybe too tepid?
Kind regards sound sincere, could I come to regret it?
Hot regards are too spicy but that could do the trick.
But if she doesn't find it funny? Oh gosh, I feel sick!

Forever yours, With love, or *Undying affection?*
Everything I think of leads in the wrong direction!
Will follow up soon seems like a threat.
I feel myself breaking into a cold sweat.

With eternal gratitude, does that make me sound meek?
Well, she was quite helpful with the printer last week.
Sending good vibes, I might as well quit.
Doesn't she have that conference, maybe *Have a good trip*?

All the best is good but it is a bit haughty.
XOXO is simply too naughty.
Ta-ta for now seems awfully silly.
Ciao is sweet and simple, but comes across willy-nilly.

Take care means I love her; *Cheers* is obtuse.
Stay safe sounds like a killer's on the loose.
Might as well go with *Goodbye* in the end.
Oh wait, did I just press *Send*?

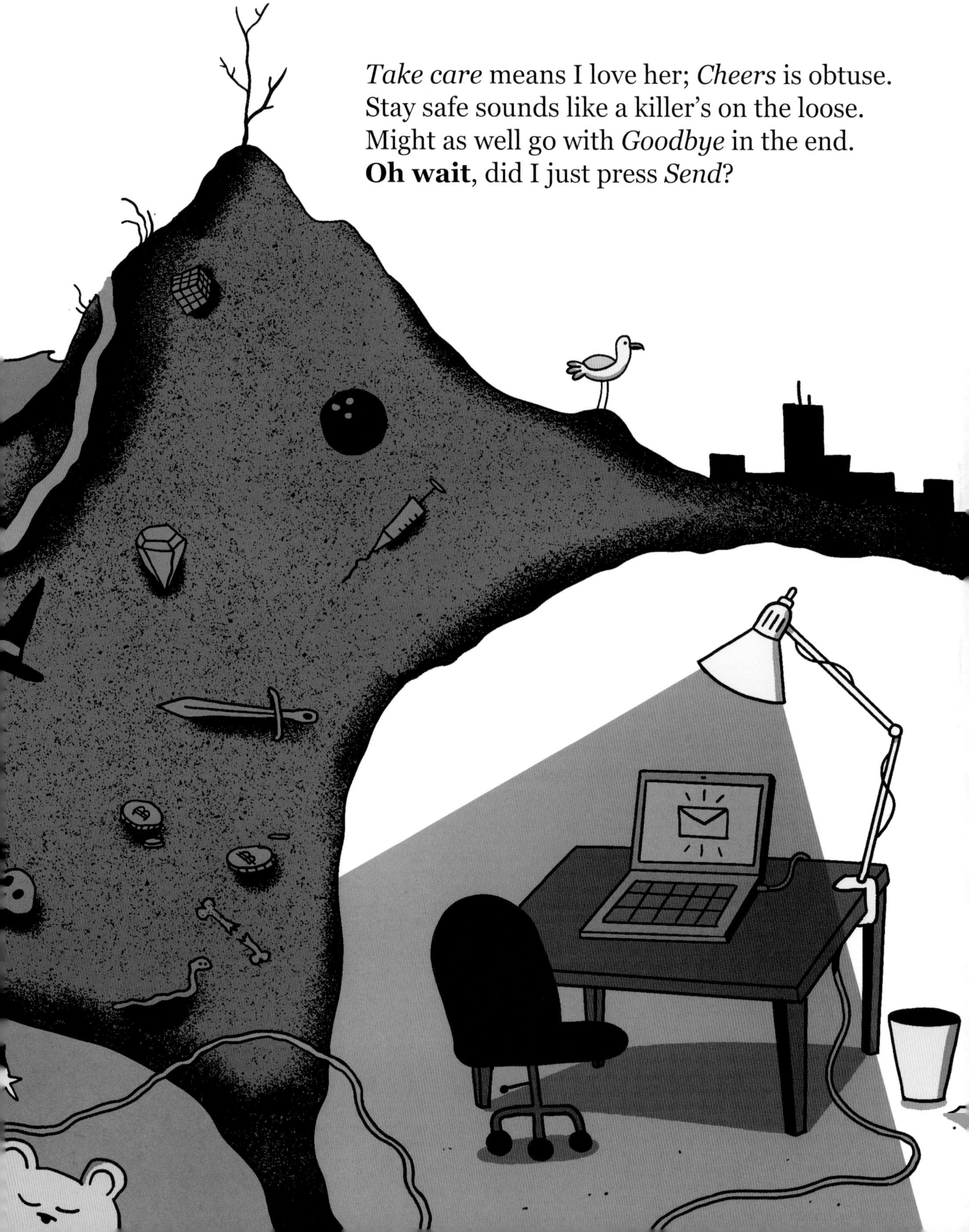

Clown Life

Every morning at eight, I paint on my face
The clownmobile swings by at nine
I'm the preacher of pranks, I know my place
To serve the relief for which they pine

My tie may be crooked, my shoes too big
On really bad days there are fleas in my wig
But a clown must make do, like a cow must go moo
And just keep on soothing humanity's blues

When I went to clown college, they said it'd be rough
Some days your crowd will be listless and gruff
You might dance for some kids who forgot how to smile
Then they'll laugh and feel all right for a while

After the show, I pack my frog and toad
My car's the one filled with red balloons
I get myself a cocoa for the road
And turn on my favorite tunes

When I get home through the gates,
Where the sadness awaits
I tell myself I'm doing God's work
I've performed for divorce lawyers, teens, and inmates
And I swear I saw some of them smirk

My sister, she worries I might blow a fuse
That one day I'll keel over in my too-big clown shoes
But laughter, I believe, is a human right
And I am here to fight that good fight.

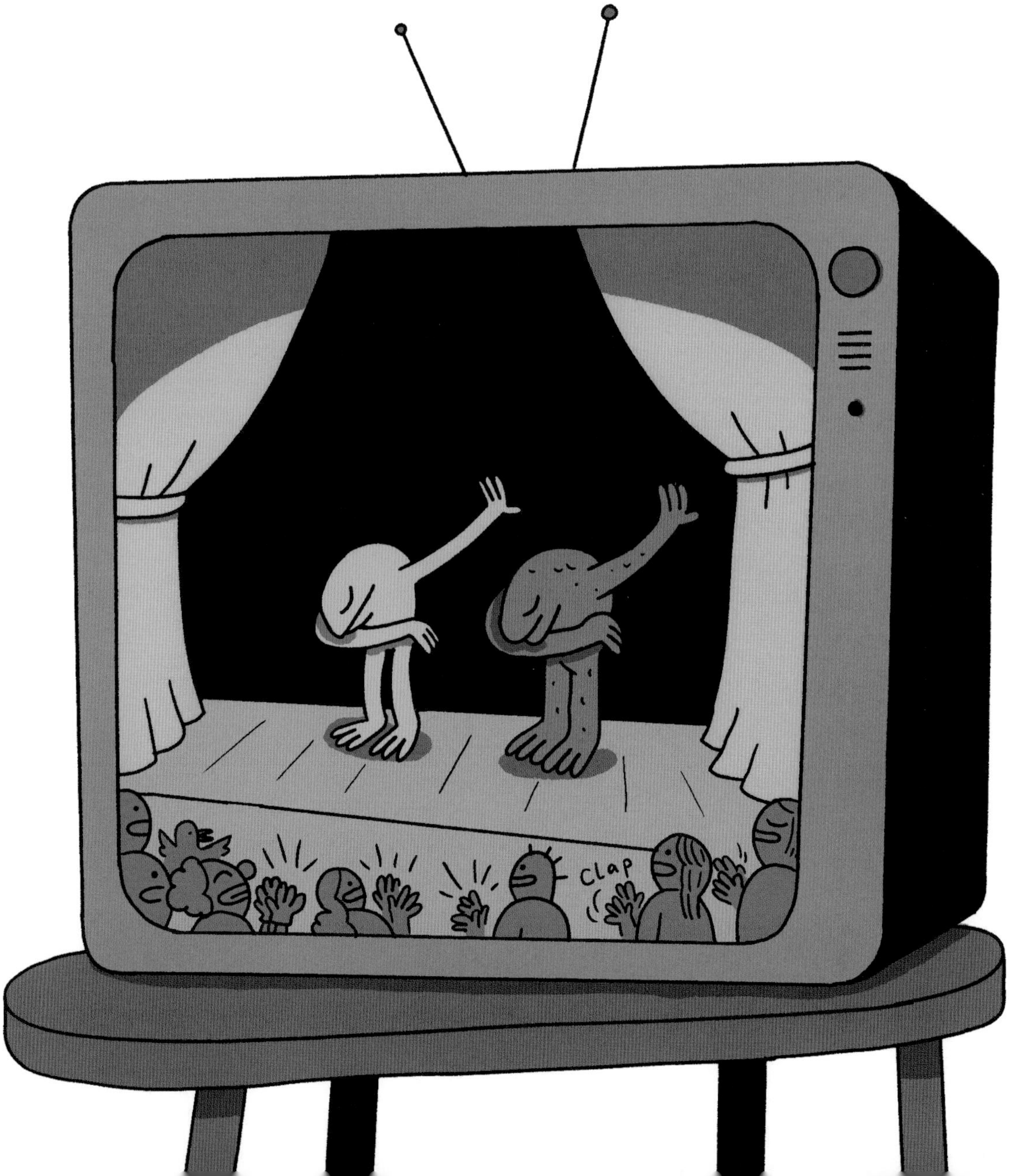
clap

Thanks

Anita Ettinger & Thomas Kunz, Eva LeWinter, Dorothea & Gunnar Kunz, Mara Sitzmann, Dennis Schank, Denise Rixecker, Mariela Georgieva, Mona Benndorf, Vasilis Plakias, Monika Romer, Wiktoria Nowogrodzka, Fabienne Stolz, Sarah Andersen, Heidi Isecke, Benjamin Garcia, Charlie Olsen, Lucas Wetzel.

Thank you to all our patrons.

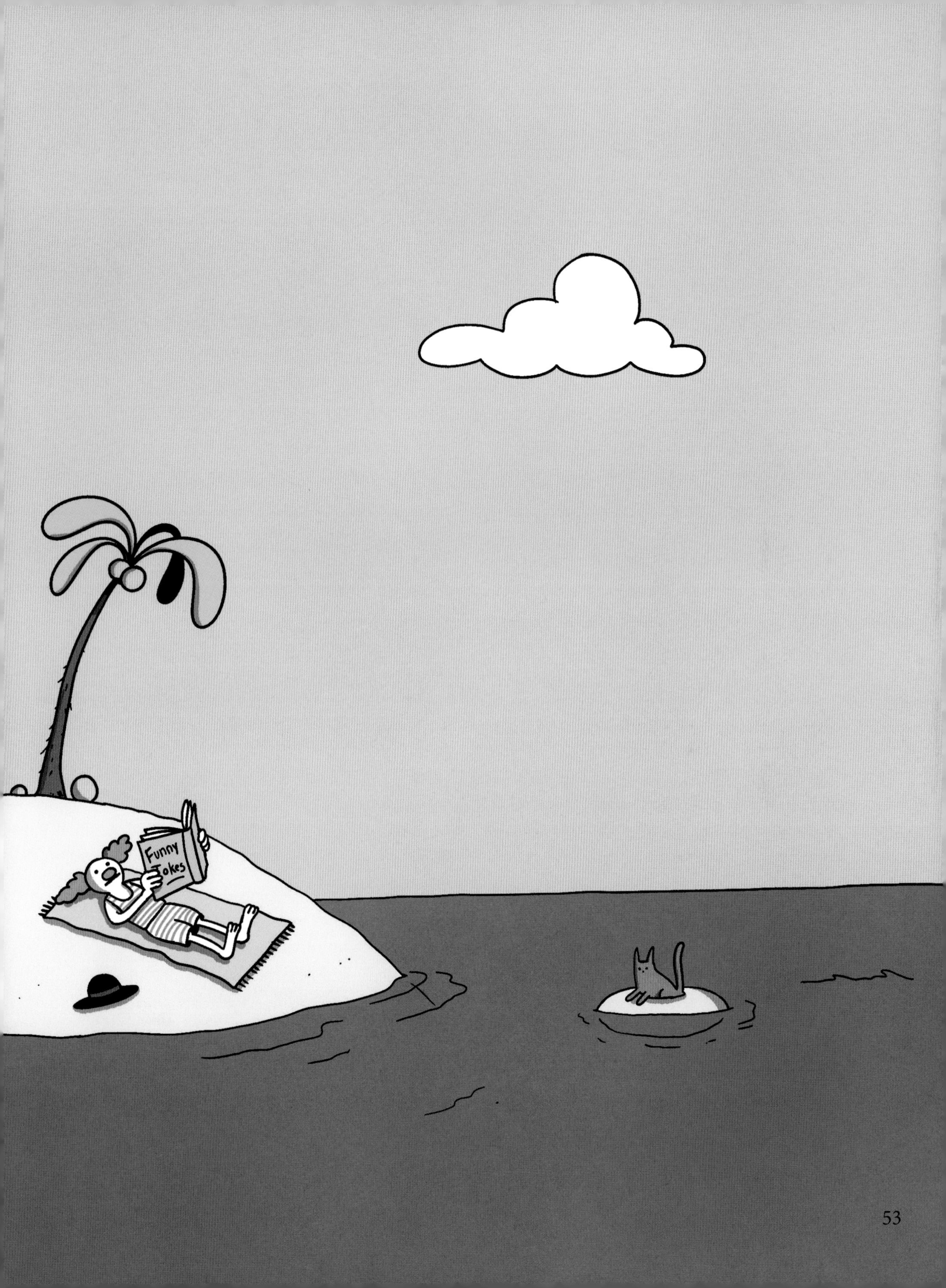
Funny Jokes

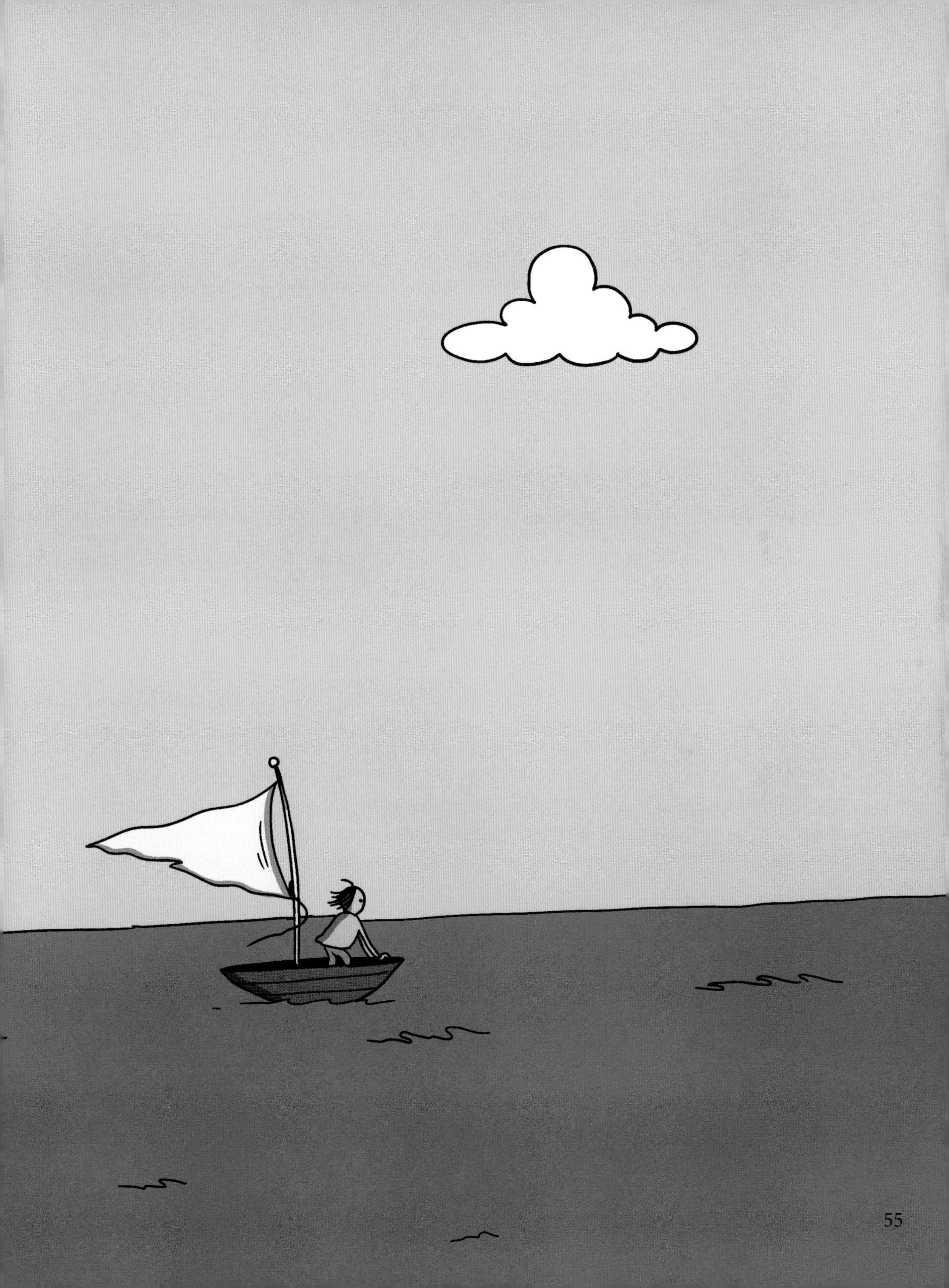

Andrews McMeel Publishing
a division of Andrews McMeel Universal
1130 Walnut Street, Kansas City, Missouri 64106

24 25 26 27 28 SDB 10 9 8 7 6 5 4 3 2 1

ISBN: 978-1-5248-8238-9

Library of Congress Control Number: 2023944315

Editor: Lucas Wetzel
Designer: Brittany Lee
Production Editor: Brianna Westervelt
Production Manager: Chadd Keim

www.andrewsmcmeel.com

www.warandpeas.com

ATTENTION: SCHOOLS AND BUSINESSES
Andrews McMeel books are available at quantity discounts with bulk purchase for educational, business, or sales promotional use. For information, please e-mail the Andrews McMeel Publishing Special Sales Department: sales@amuniversal.com.